THIS IS
BERLIN

B/S

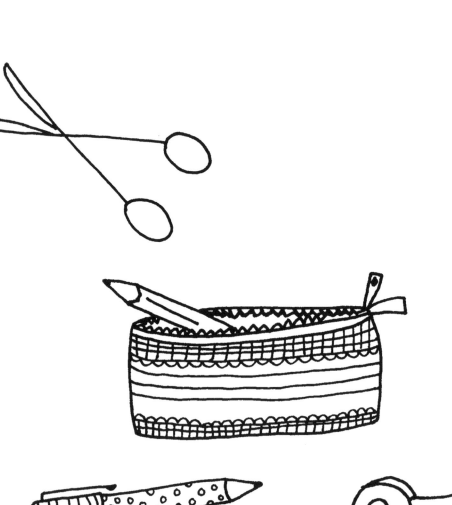

THIS BOOK BELONGS TO

DATE

DU BIST VERRÜC[

DU MUSST NACH

MEIN KIND,
BERLIN.

FRANZ VON SUPPÉ

Things I would like to see and do in Berlin

MARKERS, PENS, PENCILS & TUBES OF PAINT

MODULOR
Prinzenstraße 85
10969 Berlin-Kreuzberg

CYM
Diepenbachstraße 16
Planufer 96
10967 Berlin-Kreuzberg

KÜNSTLERMAGAZIN
Kastanienallee 33
10435 Berlin-Prenzlauer Berg

PETERS ART SHOP
Gottschedtstraße 26
13357 Berlin-Charlottenburg

PHILOGRAPHOS GMBH
Knesebeckstraße 3
10623 Berlin-Charlottenburg

R.S.V.P.
Mulackstraße 14 & 26
10119 Berlin-Mitte

SCHOENE SCHREIBWAREN
Niederbarnimstraße 6
10247 Berlijn-Friedrichshain
Weinbergsweg 21
10119 Berlin-Mitte

U-BAHN & S-BAHN FOR PROS

Trace from a real metro map:
which U- or S-Bahn have you
taken, where did you get off, and
what are the most beautiful
names?

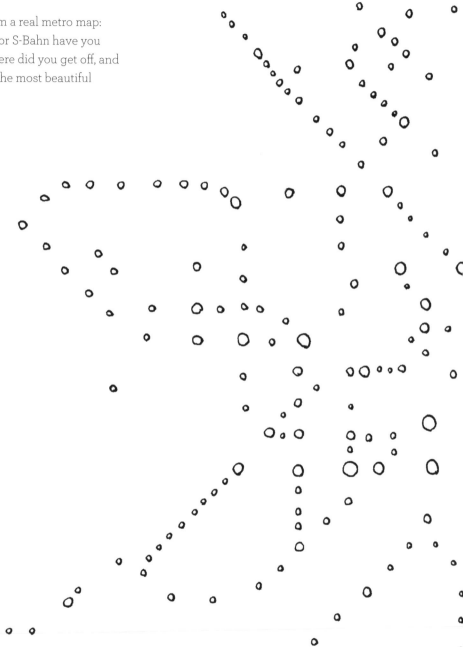

I DON'T DRINK TEA,
I TAKE COFFEE MY DEAR

TALL, DARK & BROWNIES

HIP COFFEE BARS

☐ **EAST & EDEN**
   Torstraße 141
   10119 Berlin-Mitte

☐ **THE BARN ROASTERY**
   Schönhauser Allee 8
   10119 Berlin-Mitte

☐ **BONANZA COFFEE ROASTERS**
   Oderberger Straße 35
   10435 Berlin-Prenzlauer Berg

☐ **WESTBERLIN**
   Friedrichstraße 215
   10969 Berlin-Mitte

☐ **FIVE ELEPHANT**
   Reichenbergerstraße 101
   10999 Berlin-Kreuzberg

☐ ....
☐ ....
☐ ....

KAFFEE & KUCHEN

TRADITIONAL COFFEE HOUSES

☐ **ANNA BLUME**
   Kollwitzstraße 83
   10435 Berlin-Prenzlauer Berg

☐ **CAFÉ EINSTEIN STAMMHAUS**
   Kurfürstenstraße 58
   10785 Berlin-Tiergarten

☐ **CAFÉ SAVIGNY**
   Grolmanstraße 53-54
   10623 Berlin-Charlottenburg

☐ **KONDITOREI BUCHWALD**
   Bartningallee 29
   10557 Berlin-Moabit

☐ **KAFFEEHAUS GROSZ**
   Kurfürstendamm 193-194
   10707 Berlin-Charlottenburg

☐ ....
☐ ....
☐ ....

TICKETS & BUSINESS CARDS

Add your nicest ones to this page,
or copy them in a drawing.

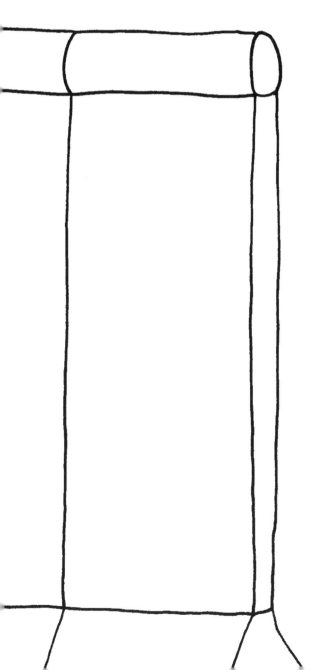

EAST SIDE GALLERY

The East Side Gallery – a part of the Berlin wall between Fried-richshain and Kreuzberg on Mühlenstraße along the Spree river – was created by artists from all over the world. The image to have been photographed most often might just be the *Fraternal Kiss* between Brezhnev and Honecker with the inscription "Mein Gott, hilf mir, diese tödliche Liebe zu überleben". The open-air gallery was opened in 1990: across the entire distance of 1.3 kilometres, 118 artists added some paint to the grey concrete blocks. But, let's be honest: some of the artwork is not actually all that good.

You can do better.

BERLIN
BREWERIES

Whether it's trendy *craft beer* or
just perfectly ordinary Berliner
Pilsner, the labels are all
appealing. Design your own label
on the second bottle.

FLOWERS, LEAVES & SHOPPING LISTS

Stick your most beautiful finds to these pages.

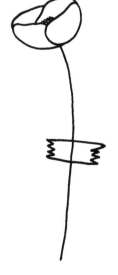

SIGHTS YOU DO NOT WANT TO MISS

Obviously, you don't have to go, but these highlights are popular for a reason. Tick them off your list!

- [ ] BRANDENBURG GATE
- [ ] BERLIN TV TOWER
- [ ] HOLOCAUST MEMORIAL
- [ ] BERLIN CATHEDRAL
- [ ] WORLD CLOCK ALEXANDERPLATZ
- [ ] KARL-MARX-ALLEE
- [ ] VICTORY COLUMN
- [ ] REICHSTAG
- [ ] MUSEUM ISLAND
- [ ] EAST SIDE GALLERY
- [ ] BERLIN WALL MEMORIAL
- [ ] POTSDAMER PLATZ
- [ ] *KAISER WILHELM MEMORIAL CHURCH*
- [ ] NEPTUNE FOUNTAIN
- [ ] OBERBAUM BRIDGE
- [ ] VIKTORIAPARK
- [ ] ....
- [ ] ....
- [ ] ....
- [ ] ....
- [ ] ....

MOLECULE MAN

Made in 1999.
Sculpture in the Spree.
30 metres in height,
45 tons in weight.

This sculpture by the American sculptor Jonathan Borofsky consists of three aluminium male figures, punctured with holes, symbolising the three districts Friedrichshain, Kreuzberg and Köpenick. On the one hand the sculpture represents the reunited Berlin, and on the other hand the artist uses the sculpture to express that people should coexist peacefully.

The sculpture can clearly be viewed from the Elsenbrücke and the Oberbaum Bridge, as it is located in between these two bridges. The most beautiful photographs of the sculpture can be taken during sunset.

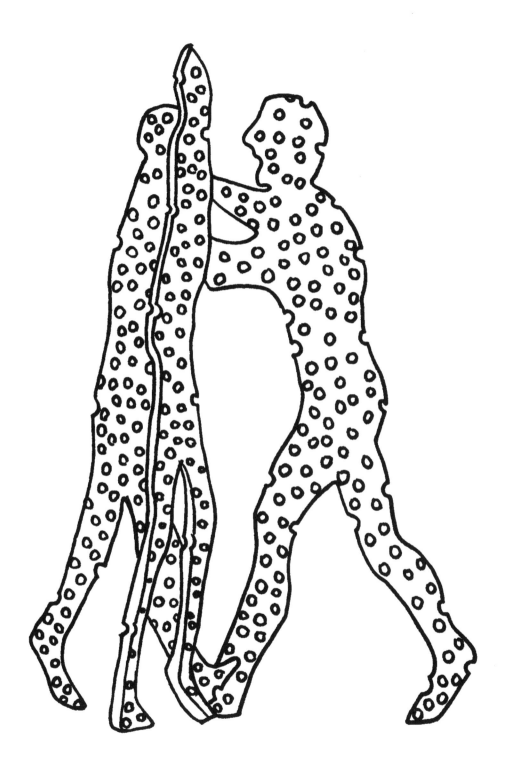

BERLIN FRIKADELLER

A tasty snack to go with your glass of beer. With a crisp pickled gherkin, a good dollop of sharp mustard and perhaps some bread on the side. They resemble Dutch meatballs, but are pressed a bit flat in the pan during frying.

400 gr. organic minced meat
150 gr. breadcrumbs
1 onion, shredded
1 egg
1 tsp. mustard
½ bundle of parsley, finely chopped
approx. 50 gr. butter

Put the minced meat in a bowl. Add the breadcrumbs, onion, egg, mustard and parsley. Add a good pinch of salt and pepper and knead the mixture well.
Make 8 – 10 medium-sized balls using the palms of your hands, and then flatten them creating thick disks. Heat the butter in a big frying pan and fry the frikadeller on both sides until they are done. Serve with pickled gherkins, mustard and some brown bread.

KREUZBERGER NÄCHTE SIND...

COCKTAIL PARTIES & DREAMS

- ☐ MOSCOW MULE
- ☐ HUGO
- ☐ APEROL SPRITZ
- ☐ GIN-TONIC
- ☐ DARK 'N' STORMY
- ☐ ....
- ☐ ....
- ☐ ....

BARS & CAFÉS

☐ **MONKEY BAR (25HOURS HOTEL)**
Budapester Straße 40
10787 Berlin-Charlottenburg

☐ **LASS UNS FREUNDE BLEIBEN**
Choriner Straße 12, 10119 Berlin-Mitte

☐ **HAIFISCHBAR**
Arndtstraße 25, 10965 Berlin-Kreuzberg

☐ **LE CROCO BLEU**
Prenzlauer Allee 242
10405 Berlin-Prenzlauer Berg

☐ **WÜRGENGEL**
Dresdener Straße 122
10999 Berlin-Kreuzberg

☐ ....

AND DANCING AFTERWARDS?

☐ **TRESOR**
Köpenicker Straße 70
10179 Berlin-Kreuzberg

☐ **LIDO**
Cuvrystraße 7, 10997 Berlin-Kreuzberg

☐ **HOUSE OF WEEKEND**
Alexanderstraße 7, 10178 Berlin-Mitte

☐ **BERGHAIN**
Rüdersdorfer Straße 70
10243 Berlin-Friedrichshain

☐ **TAUSEND**
Schiffbauerdamm 11, 10117 Berlin-Mitte

☐ ....

WEST AND EAST: THE DISTRICTS OF BERLIN

Colour the districts you have visited, you still wish to visit or where you would buy a pied-à-terre if you won the lottery. The dotted line indicates where once the wall stood.

REINICKENDORF

WEDI

SPANDAU

TIERG.

CHARLOTTENBURG

WILMERSDORF

ZEHLENDORF

STEGLITZ

Dreams, notes, thoughts

LOOKING AT ART

Of course, lists as these could run on forever, as Berlin has a wealth of splendid museums and galleries. The most important museums can be found in the district Mitte. Galleries are located all across the city. Choice overload? Search for a gallery with a yellow banana on the wall, which is the signature hallmark of the German artist Thomas Baumgärtel, who visits galleries all over the world. Tick off the places you have visited, or fill out where you have been.

4X GALLERY

☐ C|O BERLIN
   www.co-berlin.org

☐ KW INSTITUTE FOR CONTEMPORARY ART
   www.kw-berlin.de

☐ BERLINISCHE GALERIE
   www.berlinischegalerie.de

☐ JR GALLERY
   www.jrgallery.de

☐ ....

☐ ....

☐ ....

5X MUSEUM

☐ BODE-MUSEUM
   www.smb.museum

☐ GERMAN HISTORICAL MUSEUM
   www.dhm.de

☐ HAMBURGER BAHNHOF
   www.smb.museum

☐ BAUHAUS ARCHIV
   www.bauhaus.de

☐ JEWISH MUSEUM
   www.jm.berlin.de

☐ ....

☐ ....

☐ ....

BOTTLE COLLECTORS

If anything is remarkable about the streets of Berlin, it certainly is the multitude of people walking around with a bottle of beer in their hand. Not just the drifters and the grunting German Shepherd owners, but also particularly ordinary people. After work, before dinner, on sultry summer evenings, in the U-Bahn, in the park. The beers are sold at late-night shops, referred to as *Spätis*.

As soon as you've emptied your bottle, you can get your deposit back or you can opt to leave the bottle out for the so-called *Flaschensammler*. Unfortunately, there are many people throughout the city who live off of collecting bottles for the deposits. Some lampposts have special crates attached to them for this specific purpose, but you can also place your bottle below the lamppost or in another spot near a bin. Once you start paying attention to it, you'll see bottles everywhere.

STREET FOOD & IMBISS

Currywurst, check, beer in hand, check. Take it from us, Berlin offers excellent options for dining out. But a tasty hamburger or a *currywurst* every now and then... Time to tick some boxes: where did you eat what?

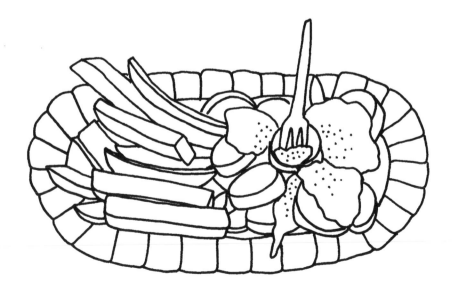

WHERE?

- [ ] Neue Heimat
  www.neueheimat.com

- [ ] Markthalle IX
  www.markthalleneun.de

- [ ] Bite Club
  www.biteclub.de

- [ ] Mustafa's Gemüse Kebap
  www.mustafas.de

- [ ] Curry 36
  www.curry36.de

- [ ] Konnopke's
  www.konnopke-imbiss.de

- [ ] Dada Falafel
  www.dadafalafel.de

- [ ] ....

- [ ] ....

WHAT?

- [ ] Döner Kebap
- [ ] Vegetable Kebap
- [ ] Hamburger
- [ ] Currywurst with/without Fries
- [ ] Kimchi Burger
- [ ] Käsespätzle
- [ ] Pulled Pork Sandwich
- [ ] Falafel

- [ ] ....

- [ ] ....

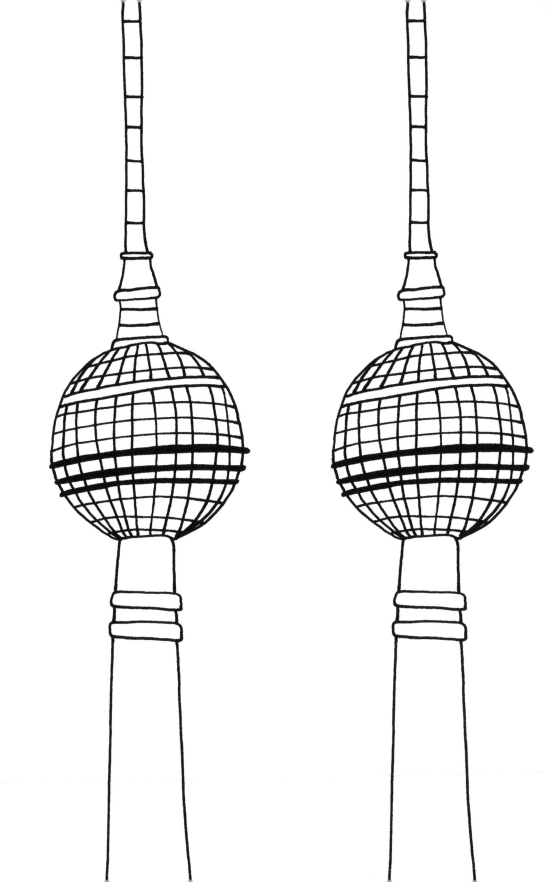

BERLIN
TV TOWER

Built in 1969.
368 metres high, panorama at a
height of 203 metres.

The tower looks different each
time and some cold, foggy days
you cannot see it at all. That's
quite a pity, because it is an
excellent orientation point when
you are making your way through
the city. During the annual Festival
of Lights, the tower lights up in
various colours. In 2006, for
instance, the silver ball was
'dressed' like a football and the
possibilities are virtually infinite.
The mast is striped in red and
white, but a rainbow might even
be a much better idea. So go
ahead and colour this much-loved
tower.

FLEA MARKETS

Take those old GDR eggcups in the shape of a rooster, those beautiful sunglasses, that camera or that splendid vintage coat back home with you. The traditional Berlin Sunday starts off with breakfast and continues with a visit to a flea market. Or, better yet, reverse the order: first buy something nice, and then enjoy an elaborate brunch.

☐ **BOXHAGENER PLATZ**
  10245 Berlin-Friedrichshain

☐ **ARKONAPLATZ**
  10435 Berlin-Prenzlauer Berg

☐ **MAUERPARK**
  Bernauer Straße 63-64
  13355 Berlin-Prenzlauer Berg

☐ **ANTIQUE MARKET AT THE BODE MUSEUM**
  Am Kupfergraben
  10117 Berlin-Mitte

☐ **NOWKOELLN (BI-WEEKLY)**
  Maybachufer 31
  12047 Berlin-Kreuzberg

☐ **BERLINER TRÖDELMARKT**
  Straße des 17. Juni 110-114
  10623 Berlin-Charlottenburg

☐ ....

☐ ....

☐ ....

The city, the people, the sounds, the smells

FILMS IN, ABOUT & FROM BERLIN

- [ ] 24 STUNDEN BERLIN – EIN TAG IM LEBEN
- [ ] DAS LEBEN DER ANDEREN
- [ ] HERR LEHMANN
- [ ] DER HIMMEL ÜBER BERLIN
- [ ] OH BOY
- [ ] GOOD BYE, LENIN!
- [ ] CHRISTIANE F.
- [ ] SONNENALLEE
- [ ] THE INVISIBLE FRAME
- [ ] MEIN LANGSAMES LEBEN
- [ ] SOMMER VORM BALKON
- [ ] LOLA RENNT
- [ ] WEISSENSEE
- [ ] ....
- [ ] ....
- [ ] ....

CITY SOUNDS

- ☐ HONKING TAXIS
- ☐ RINGING CYCLISTS
- ☐ BIRDS ON THE TERRACE
- ☐ SQUEAKING TRAMS IN THE BEND
- ☐ SCREAMING TODDLERS IN THE PLAYGROUND
- ☐ TECHNO, TECHNO, TECHNO
- ☐ CONSTRUCTION WORKERS
- ☐ GRAVEL STUCK TO YOUR SOLES IN WINTER
- ☐ ....
- ☐ ....
- ☐ ....

98014 DOGS

It seems as though everyone in Berlin has a dog. Either the latest it-dog (a pug), a frayed shepherd, a perilous-looking fight dog or a neatly groomed poodle. However, the dog population in the entire city ultimately amounts to no more than 100,000 and that actually doesn't sound so extreme when you take the city's 3.5 million inhabitants into consideration.

ZURÜCKBLEIBEN BITTE!

There are so many beautiful U-Bahn stations that some people make a sport out of photographing them all. Cross out the ones where you got on or off the U-Bahn. Or the ones you have past along the way.

Adenauerplatz
Afrikanische Straße
Alexanderplatz
Alt-Mariendorf
Alt-Tegel
Alt-Tempelhof
Altstadt Spandau
Amrumer Straße
Augsburger Straße
Bayerischer Platz
Berliner Straße
Bernauer Straße
Biesdorf-Süd
Birkenstraße
Bismarckstraße
Blaschkoallee
Blissestraße
Boddinstraße
Borsigwerke
Breitenbachplatz
Brandenburger Tor
Britz-Süd
Bülowstraße
Bundestag
Bundesplatz
Cottbusser Platz
Dahlem-Dorf
Deutsche Oper
Eberswalder Straße
Eisenacher Straße
Elsterwerdaer Platz
Ernst-Reuter-Platz
Fehrbelliner Platz
Frankfurter Allee
Frankfurter Tor
Franz-Neumann-Platz
Französische Straße
Friedrichsfelde
Friedrichstraße
Friedrich-Wilhelm-Platz
Gesundbrunnen
Gleisdreieck
Gneisenaustraße
Görlitzer Bahnhof

Grenzallee
Güntzelstraße
Halemweg
Hallesches Tor
Hansaplatz
Haselhorst
Hauptbahnhof
Hausvogteiplatz
Heidelberger Platz
Heinrich-Heine-Straße
Hellersdorf
Hermannplatz
Hermannstraße
Hönow
Hohenzollernplatz
Holzhauser Straße
Innsbrucker Platz
Jakob-Kaiser-Platz
Jannowitzbrücke
Johannisthaler Chaussee
Jungfernheide
Kaiserdamm
Kaiserin-Augusta-Straße
Karl-Bonhoeffer-Nerven-
klinik
Karl-Marx-Straße
Kaulsdorf-Nord
Kleistpark
Klosterstraße
Kochstraße
Konstanzer Straße
Kottbusser Tor
Krumme Lanke
Kurfürstendamm
Kurfürstenstraße
Kurt-Schumacher-Platz
Leinestraße
Leopoldplatz
Lichtenberg
Lindauer Allee
Lipschitzallee
Louis-Lewin-Straße
Magdalenenstraße
Märkisches Museum

Mehringdamm
Mendelssohn-Barthol-
dy-Park
Mierendorffplatz
Möckernbrücke
Mohrenstraße
Moritzplatz
Naturkundemuseum
Nauener Platz
Neu-Westend
Neue Grottkauer Straße
Neukölln
Nollendorfplatz
Olympia-Stadion
Onkel Toms Hütte
Oranienburger Tor
Oskar-Helene-Heim
Osloer Straße
Otisstraße
Pankow
Pankstraße
Paracelsus-Bad
Paradestraße
Parchimer Allee
Paulsternstraße
Platz der Luftbrücke
Podbielskiallee
Potsdamer Platz
Prinzenstraße
Rathaus Neukölln
Rathaus Reinickendorf
Rathaus Schöneberg
Rathaus Spandau
Rathaus Steglitz
Rehberge
Reinickendorfer Straße
Residenzstraße
Richard-Wagner-Platz
Rohrdamm
Rosa-Luxemburg-Platz
Rosenthaler Platz
Rüdesheimer Platz
Rudow
Ruhleben

Samariterstraße
Scharnweberstraße
Schillingstraße
Schlesisches Tor
Schloßstraße
Schönhauser Allee
Schönleinstraße
Schwartzkopffstraße
Seestraße
Senefelderplatz
Siemensdamm
Sophie-Charlotte-Platz
Spichernstraße
Spittelmarkt
Stadtmitte
Strausberger Platz
Südstern
Tempelhof
Theodor-Heuss-Platz
Thielplatz
Tierpark
Turmstraße
Uhlandstraße
Ullsteinstraße
Viktoria-Luise-Platz
Vinetastraße
Voltastraße
Walther-Schreiber-Platz
Warschauer Straße
Weberwiese
Wedding
Weinmeisterstraße
Westhafen
Westphalweg
Wilmersdorfer Straße
Wittenau
Wittenbergplatz
Wuhletal
Wutzkyallee
Yorckstraße
Zitadelle
Zoologischer Garten
Zwickauer Damm

THEATRE, OPERA & TRADITIONAL MUSIC

The lobbies of these venues are particularly good for people watching, but of course they also offer beautiful plays and concerts.

☐ **KOMISCHE OPER**
Behrenstraße 55-57, 10117 Berlin-Mitte
www.komische-oper-berlin.de

☐ **VOLKSBÜHNE**
Rosa-Luxemburg-Platz, 10178 Berlin-Mitte
www.volksbuehne-berlin.de

☐ **BERLINER ENSEMBLE**
Bertolt-Brecht-Platz 1, 10117 Berlin-Mitte
www.berliner-ensemble.de

☐ **MAXIM GORKI THEATRE**
Am Festungsgraben 2, 10117 Berlin-Mitte
www.gorki.de

☐ **BERLINER PHILHARMONIE**
Herbert-von-Karajan-Straße 1,
10785 Berlin-Tiergarten
www.berliner-philharmoniker.de

☐ ....

☐ ....

☐ ....

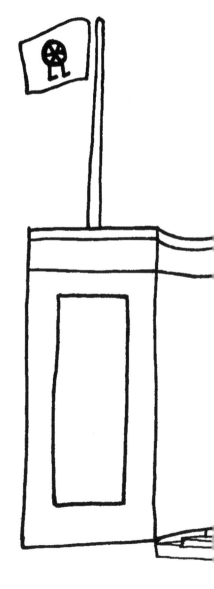

TODAY
WE'LL DO
ABSOLUTELY
NOTHING

REICHSTAG / BUNDESTAG

The flag at the entrance was raised on 3 October 1990, the day of German Unity, and has been hanging there day and night ever since. It was not until 1999 that the parliament officially relocated from Bonn to the Platz der Republik in Mitte. The name can sometimes be confusing: the Reichstag is the seat of the parliament, which is in turn referred to as the Bundestag.

Spots I have visited and wish to remember

WORLD CLOCK ALEXANDERPLATZ

These destinations are really all represented on this beautiful 'Weltzeituhr'.
From Accra to Wolgograd: cross out the places you have been.

Accra	Daressalam	Lisbon	Quito
Addis Abeba	Dawson	London	Rangun
Aden	Denver Dhaka	Los Angeles	Reykjavik
Almaty	Dublin	Machadan	Riga
Amsterdam	Duschanbe	Madeira	Rio de Janeiro
Anchorage	Edmonton	Madrid	Rome
Ankara	Eriwan	Managua	Sachalin
Antananarivo	Fairbanks	Manila	San Francisco
Apia	Galápagos	Marquesas	Sanaa
Aschagabat	Guatemala City	Mauritius	Santa Fé de Bogota
Asunción	Halifax	Melbourne	Santiago de Chile
Athens	Hanoi	Mexico City	Sao Paulo
Azores	Havana	Minsk	Seoul
Bagdad	Helsinki	Mogadischu	Shanghai
Baku	Hong Kong	Montevideo	Singapur
Bamako	Honolulu	Montreal	Sofi
Bangkok	Irkutsk Istanbul	Moscow	St.Petersburg
Beirut	Jakarta	Murmansk	Stockholm
Belgrade	Jakutsk	New Delhi	Sydney
Berlin	Jekaterinburg	New Orleans	Tallinn
Bern	Jerusalem	New York	Taschkent
Bischkek	Kabul	Nikosia	Teheran
Bissau	Cairo	Nischnij Nowogorod	Tel Aviv
Brazil	Kamtschatka	Nome	Tiflis
Brussels	Cape Dezhnev	Nowosibirsk	Tokyo
Budapest	Cape Verde	Omsk	Tunis
Buenos Aires	Cape Town	Oslo	Ulan-Bator
Bukarest	Karachi	Østgrønland	Vancouver
Canberra	Kiev	Panama	Warsaw
Caracas	Kinshasa	Paris	Washington
Casablanca	Copenhagen	Beijing	Wellington
Chabarowsk	Krasnojarsk	Perth	Westgrønland
Colombo	Kuala Lumpur	Phnom Penh	Vienna
Conakry	Kuwait	Pjöngjang	Wilna
Dakar	La Paz	Prague	Wladiwostok
Damascus	Lima	Pressburg	Wolgograd

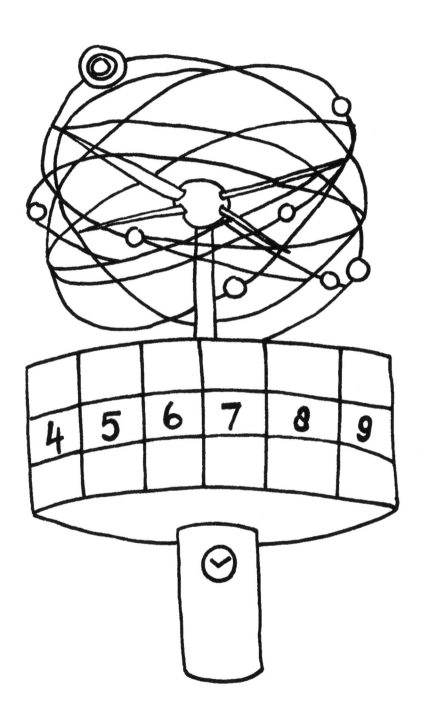

2 EUROS, 5-MINUTE WAIT, 4 PHOTOS

Add your own photo strip from the photo booth on this page.

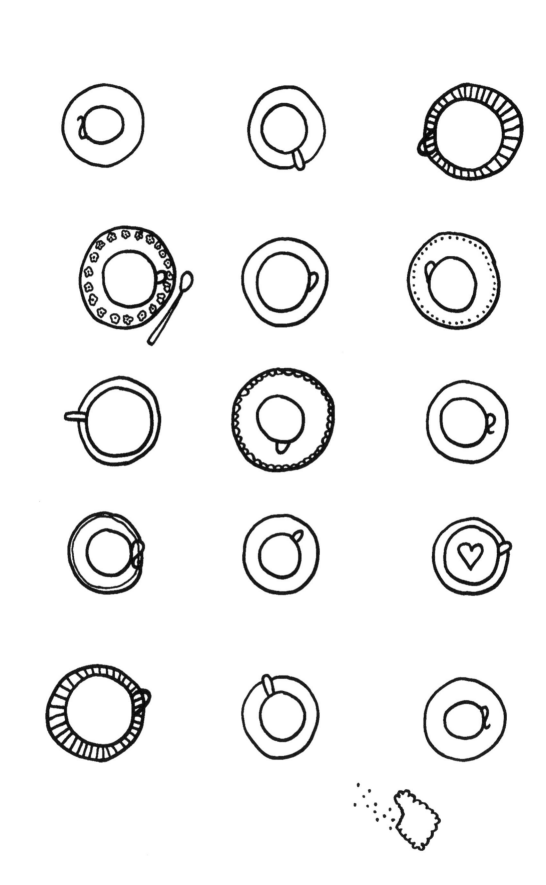

I HAVE A PHD IN LATTE ART

Hearts, leaves, the Brandenburg Gate: draw your own latte art in the milk foam of these cappuccinos.

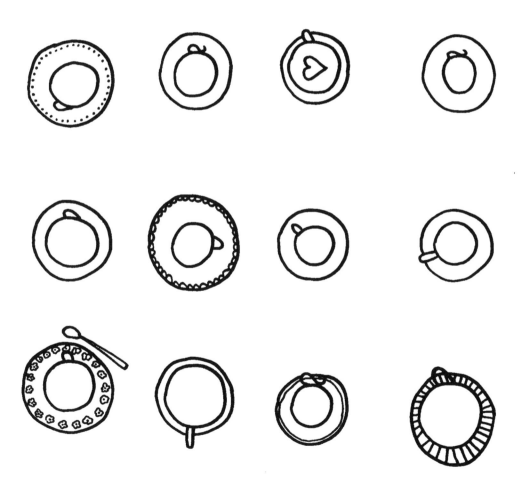

TODAY IS GOING TO BE A GREAT DAY

Go for a picnic in the park, cycle part of the Berlin Wall Trail, or discover one of the many lakes in Brandenburg and have a swim. Delightful! Going for a bike ride is cooling and you can visit the outskirts of the city. Rent a bicycle and go out to explore.

BOOKSHOPS THAT MAKE YOU HAPPY

☐ **HUNDT HAMMER STEIN**
Alte Schönhauser Straße 24
10119 Berlin-Mitte

☐ **REISEBUCHHANDLUNG SCHROPP**
Hardenbergstraße 9a
10623 Berlin-Charlottenburg

☐ **DUSSMANN DAS KULTURKAUFHAUS**
Friedrichstraße 90
10117 Berlin-Mitte

☐ **PRO QM**
Almstadtstraße 48-50
10119 Berlin-Mitte

☐ **BÜCHERBOGEN AM SAVIGNYPLATZ**
Stadtbahnbogen 593
10623 Berlin-Charlottenburg

☐ **BUCHBOX! KIEZBUCHHANDLUNG**
multiple locations in the city
www.buchboxberlin.de

☐ **KOHLHAAS & COMPANY**
Fasanenstraße 23
10719 Berlin-Charlottenburg

☐ **ONKEL & ONKEL**
Oranienstraße 195
10999 Berlin-Kreuzberg

☐ ....

☐ ....

☐ ....

AND FOR THE MOST BEAUTIFUL MAGAZINES YOU CAN VISIT

☐ **DO YOU READ ME?!**
Auguststraße 28, 10117 Berlin-Mitte

☐ ....

☐ ....

☐ ....

BOOKS ON BERLIN

☐ **ALFRED DÖBLIN**
Berlin Alexanderplatz

☐ **HANS FALLADA**
Alone in Berlin

☐ **JUDITH HERMANN**
The summer house, later

☐ **OTTO DE KAT**
News from Berlin

☐ **CHLOE ARIDJIS**
Book of Clouds

☐ **CEES NOOTEBOOM**
Roads to Berlin

☐ **SVEN REGENER**
Berlin Blues

☐ **ANNA FUNDER**
Stasiland

☐ **THOMAS BRUSSIG**
Heroes Like Us

☐ ....

☐ ....

☐ ....

TALL PEOPLE, SHORT PEOPLE, FAT PEOPLE, SKINNY PEOPLE

Who is sitting across from you in the U-Bahn? Draw them!

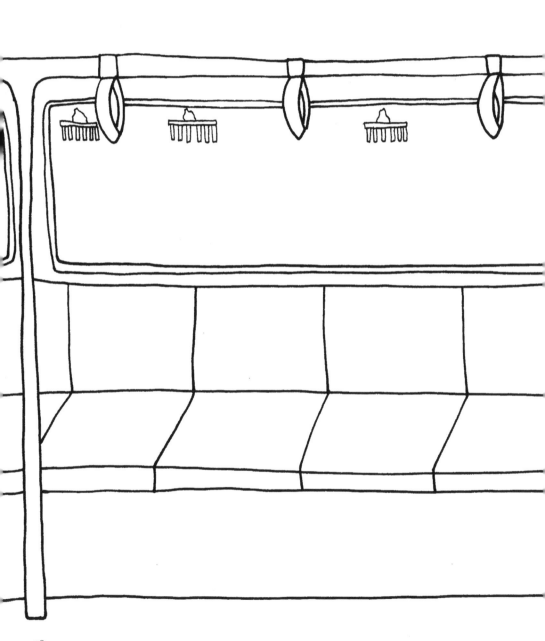

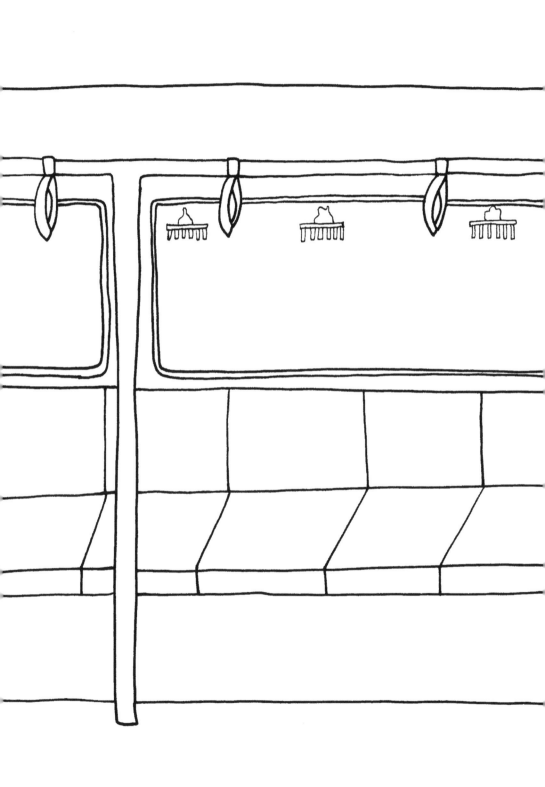

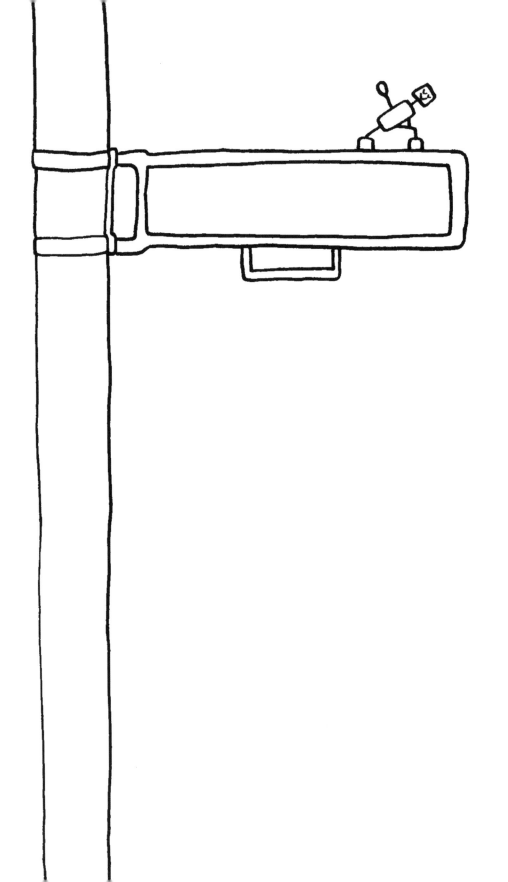

STREETS OF BERLIN

Look up at the street signs, because you might just be lucky enough to spot one of the many Street Yogis. Small figures made from cork and sticks, high above the pavement. There are approximately 1000 figures to be spotted, especially in Mitte, Kreuzberg and Neukölln.
In a yoga posture! The idea came from a yoga teacher in the city. He placed the first ones, but in the meantime others have started to make them as well. The little figures are supposed to bring luck and joy. Especially if you just leave them where they are.

Just your luck: not able to find a single Street Yogi? Then at least you can search for the most beautiful street names of the city, such as the Allee der Kosmonauten. Or fill out the name of the street where you spent the night.

ERNST THÄLMANN MEMORIAL

In the former East Berlin you will see huge sculptures here and there, often showing Russian soldiers. This sculpture is located on Greifswalder Straße. Ernst Thälmann was the leader of the communist party KPD in Germany and was honoured in the GDR with sculptures such as this one.

ROTFRONT ERNS

DEUTSCH IST EINE SCHÖNE SPRACHE!

However, the colloquial Berlin dialect is a true joy. No hassle with pesky throat sounds when trying to pronounce "ich": just a straightforward "ick" does the trick. Unfortunately, it can sometimes be very hard to understand the local dialect, but it certainly is fun to listen to.

BETTER THAN A TEXT MESSAGE

Below, note down the names of five people, buy five postcards and five stamps, and then write five beautiful sentences on each card.
Do not forget to post.

KITSCH & ART

Take a picture of the ugliest souvenirs you encounter and stick the photographs on this page. Or draw them. Our favourite: the juicer with Angela Merkel's head.

Life is too short to learn german

BERLINER LUFT

Ah, the famous *Berliner Luft*. No, not the drink, nor the smell of the city, but an old-fashioned desert. If only because of its name, you should make this at least once.

2 sheets of gelatin
2 very fresh eggs
3 tbs. sugar
grater & juice of ½ lemon
50 ml sparkling or white wine
200 gr. raspberries

Soak the sheets of gelatin in cold water. Separate the eggs. Beat the egg yolks with sugar until they are creamy and add the grated lemon peel and some lemon juice. Heat the wine in a small pan, take off the fire and let the gelatin dissolve in it.

Let it cool and set aside. Beat the egg whites with a pinch of salt until stiff peaks form. Carefully fold the egg whites into the egg yolks.

Divide into 4-6 glasses and place in the fridge for at least 1 hour. Purée the raspberries (add some water, if necessary), push through a sieve and garnish the *Luft* with this raspberry sauce.

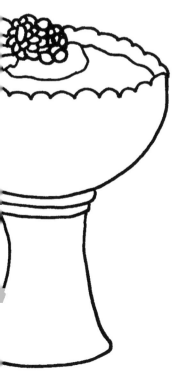

MY 8 MOST BEAUTIFUL PHOTOS

Print out in 5 x 5 cm and stick them here. Just like a real Polaroid!

BARGAINS & BAD BUYS

Regretting that one jacket that you left behind? If only you could have just kept yourself from buying those expensive trousers.
Draw your bad buys, your bargains and your missed purchases here.

BRANDENBURGER TOR

Built in 1788-1791.
26 metres in height,
65.5 metres wide.
On 22 December 1989, it was
finally opened again for East
and West Berliners.

Each year, some 11 million tourists
come to Berlin. We have not yet
met many who did not at least
want to 'quickly go through' the
former city gate in between
Unter den Linden and Straße des
17. Juni. Truly: we estimate the
number of selfies taken with the
Brandenburg Gate at a rough 10.9
million.

ROOM WITH A VIEW

Draw the view from your window.

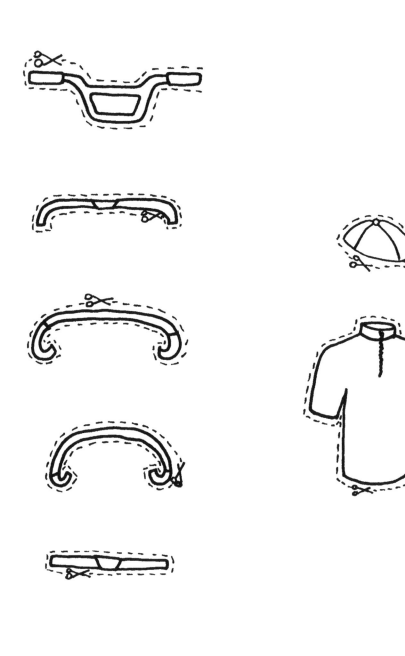

FIX YOUR FIXIE

Yes, cool, a hip city bike. With or without brakes, in gold and white or bright pink and orange.
The handlebars are very, very important: narrow, straight or bent. And then there's the saddle. Made from expensive English leather that cannot withstand the rain or maybe rather a nice plastic one after all.
The bicycle as an accessory rather than a means of transport, we love it.

BUY LESS, CHOOSE WELL

When the wall was still standing, you could find the Kaufhaus des Westens (KaDeWe) on the West side and Centrum Warenhaus (now Galeria Kaufhof) on the East side. Those two department stores still exist. In the meantime, however, the options have somewhat expanded; you can now also visit one of the many concept stores and shopping malls across the city.

DEPARTMENT STORES & MALLS

☐ **KADEWE**
Tauentzienstraße 21-24
10789 Berlin-Schöneberg

☐ **GALERIA KAUFHOF**
Alexanderplatz 9
10178 Berlin-Mitte

☐ **BIKINI BERLIN**
Budapester Straße 38-50
10787 Berlin-Tiergarten

☐ **GALERIES LAFAYETTE BERLIN**
Friedrichstraße 76-78
10117 Berlin-Mitte

☐ ....
☐ ....
☐ ....

CONCEPT STORES

☐ **VOO STORE BERLIN**
Oranienstraße 24
10999 Berlin-Kreuzberg

☐ **SIMON&ME**
Fidicinstraße 17
10965 Berlin-Kreuzberg

☐ **GESTALTEN SPACE**
Sophie-Gips-Höfe
Sophienstraße 21
10178 Berlin-Mitte

☐ **SÜPER STORE**
Dieffenbachstraße 12
10967 Berlin-Kreuzberg

☐ **URBAN OUTFITTERS**
Weinmeisterstraße 10
10178 Berlin-Mitte

☐ ....
☐ ....
☐ ....

SUMMER SCHORLE

A much-loved summer drink is *Apfelschorle*: half sparkling mineral water, half apple juice. Its varieties are endless, and fresh herbs also make it wonderfully refreshing.

RHUBARB-WATERMELON-BASIL

2 parts mineral water
2 parts rhubarb juice
1 small, long piece of watermelon, without the peel & seeds
1 sprig of basil
ice cubes

Pour the water and the juice into a glass. Add watermelon and basil and serve with ice cubes.

WHITE WINE-LEMON-VERBENA

2 parts mineral water
2 parts white wine or grape juice
1 slice of lemon
3 leaves of verbena
ice cubes

Pour the water and the wine into a glass. Add lemon and verbena and serve with ice cubes.

ELDERBERRY-STRAWBERRY-MINT

2 parts mineral water
1 part elderberry juice
1 part strawberry juice
2 sprigs of mint
ice cubes

Pour the water and the juice into a glass. Add mint and serve with ice cubes.

LONG LIVE THE LINEN BAG

Linen bags – together with a woollen hat, cool short boots or pretty sneakers, skinny jeans and a green, half-long parka – belong to every Berliner's standard gear.
To go grocery shopping at an organic store, or for transporting your laptop. Go for a nice one, for instance from the Mauerpark flea market or at the well-known magazine store Do you read me?!! Or design your own.

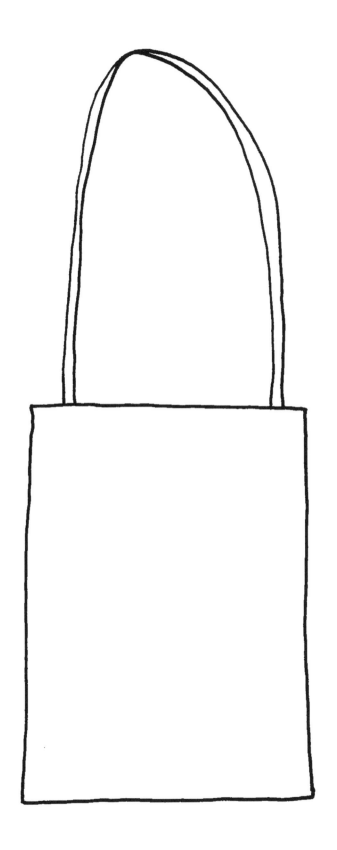

OBERBAUM BRIDGE

This beautiful bridge across the Spree river (built in between 1894 and 1902) connects Kreuzberg and Friedrichshain. Two city gates from Brandenburg served as a model for the 34-metre-high towers: one from Prenzlau, the other from Kyritz. Since 1998, the bridge has been the stage for the *Gemüseschlacht* (also known as *Wasserschlacht*) nearly every year, during which inhabitants of Friedrichshain and Kreuzberg compete against each other for the bridge, with the help of anything soft, slippery and mushy, not to mention smelly. The bridge consists of red brick, as a result of which the stripes on the towers are hardly noticeable. But that can be changed: go ahead and get creative.

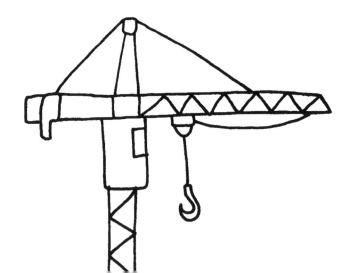

OVER THE BERLIN ROOFTOPS

Draw the view over the city as seen from the Berlin TV Tower, Bikini Berlin, Potsdamer Platz or any other high point. The crane you have undoubtedly spotted, you can now leave out.

BLA-BLA-BLA

About her new lover. On his boss.
About the annoying children.
On her new coat, which is truly
hideous. Have you heard about so
and so yet, who is doing this and
that?
Record them, those shameless
conversations. Or only note down
the most beautiful quotes.

Inspiration for at home, at work, on holidays, the rest of my life

TYPICAL BERLIN

Print your photos on 5 x 5 cm and
stick them in. Just like a real
Polaroid!

PEOPLE WATCHING

From the terrace, during hiking or cycling, or from a bench in the museum: Draw the most interesting characters you've encountered here.

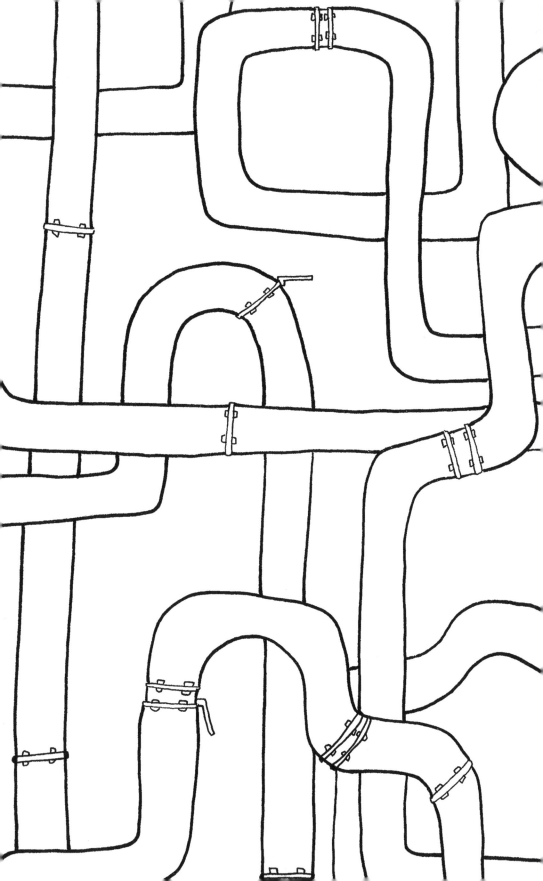

THAT PIPE AGAIN

Pink and blue pipes, high above the pavements and streets. Berlin is one big construction pit, but is also built on an old swamp. The groundwater level is very high, and at every construction site the water needs to be pumped out. That's what flows through those temporary pipes. If you follow the pipes, you will reach a construction site on one end and water on the other.

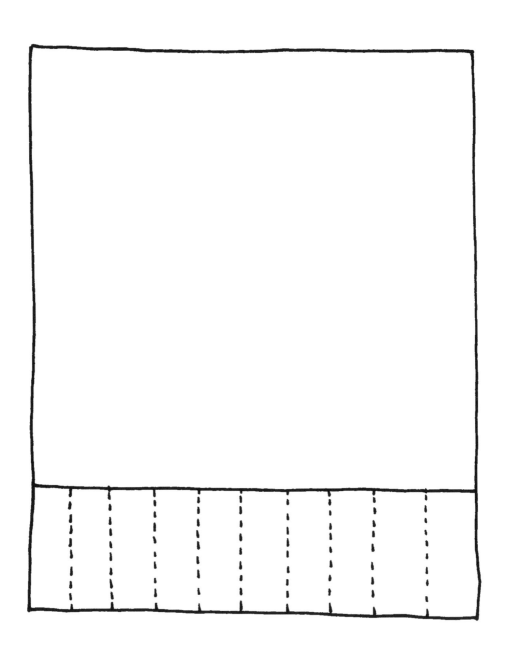

LOST
FOUND

The lampposts are covered with them; signs that in other countries you would usually find in supermarkets. Found cats, lost house keys, "Hi there, sweet stranger" letters; there are advertisements for everything. Then there are some really fun ones, too, such as the "Ohrwurm Zum Mitnehmen": one of these songs that stick in your head. Make your own sign here, cut it out and stick it on a lamppost somewhere in the city.

MISSING!

♡ SIMONE ♡
bitte melde
Dich, weil
Du die
große LIEBE
meines Leben
bist! ♡ Julius

OHRWURM
ZUM
MITNEHMEN

LIFE
IS
LIFE

18 PAIRS OF GLASSES, BEARDS, BUNS, HATS, SUMMER FRECKLES & MOHAWKS: GET CREATIVE!

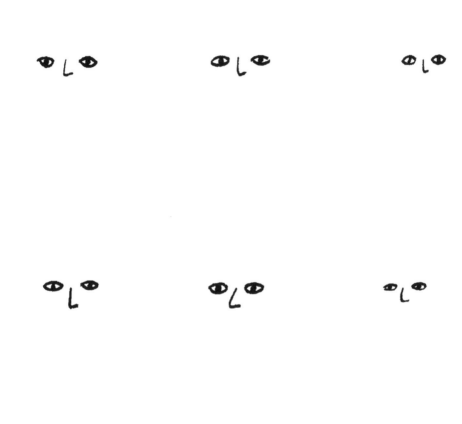

Next time I'm in Berlin...

20-21 GRAFFITI
This part of the wall is still standing in Kreuzberg, at the Schlesische Straße/Cuvry Straße corner. The graffiti was covered by black paint at the end of 2014 upon instruction from the artist. You choose: colour it or make it black.

66-67 HAUS DES LEHRERS
Facade decoration of this building near Alexanderplatz on the corner of Grünerstraße/Karl Marx Allee.

88-89 LANDWEHRKANAL
Summery scenes in Kreuzberg.

COLOPHON

ILLUSTRATIONS Anne van Haasteren
TEXT & COMPILATION Petra de Hamer
CO-AUTHOR Kim Snijders
DESIGN Oranje Vormgevers

THIS IS MY BERLIN
isbn 978-90-6369-396-1

B/SPUBLISHERS

© Text by Petra de Hamer and illustrated by Anne van Haasteren
© English edition: BIS Publishers, Amsterdam, July 2015
© Original edition: Uitgeverij Mo'Media bv, Breda, The Netherlands, www.momedia.nl

This publication has been compiled with the utmost care.
BIS Publishers cannot be held liable for any inadequacies in the text.
Any comments can be addressed to:
BIS Publishers, Building Het Sieraad, Postjesweg 1, 1057 DT Amsterdam,
info@bispublishers.nl. www.bispublishers.nl